The Art of Negotiation

Effective Strategies To Influence Human Behavior, Learn Getting to Yes without Giving In, and Become a Negotiation Genius

Nick Anderson

nick.andersonwrites@gmail.com

Table of Contents

Introduction 3
Chapter 1: What Makes a Skillful Negotiator Anyway? 14
Chapter 2: Why Negotiation Skills Are So Important? 38
Chapter 3: 7 Sure-Fire Strategies To Master Negotiation 47
Chapter 4: Anyone Can Learn Superior Bargaining Power 51
Chapter 5: How to Control the Terms of Any Negotiation 66
Chapter 6: Establish Mutual Comfort To Win Big 77
Chapter 7: How Right Mood During Negotiations Does All Magic 87
Chapter 8: Create an Anchor and Make that First Impression 96
Chapter 9: How to Frame Your Offer the Right Way 104
Chapter 10: The Best Time To Give A Counter-Offer 116
Conclusion 123

Introduction

Whether we're talking about your relationships, your job, or your business, the ability to negotiate is absolutely crucial. You may be thinking that negotiation makes a lot of sense in a business setting but nowhere else. That's not true. If you work for somebody, and you're looking for a raise or you'd like a promotion, you'd better know how to negotiate; otherwise, people can and will step all over you.

Please understand that it's a dog-eat-dog world out there. There's a tremendous amount of competition and, as the old saying goes, "The squeaky wheel gets the grease." That old saying usually involves people who complain, but that it can also apply to people who know how to draw attention and negotiate their way to a better position. Let's put it this way, if you don't ask, you probably will not receive. It's that simple.

This also applies to your relationships. If you're with somebody who you really care about, whether it's your parents or your significant other, chances are they may take you from granted. They may say things that rub you the wrong way and if you don't know how to negotiate your relationship with them, don't be surprised if you're usually frustrated or you feel that you're not getting the respect that you deserve. No matter how you cut it, you're far from fully happy.

Please understand that this is really sad because these are the people who are supposed to make you happy. These are people who are nearest and dearest to you. Do you see the disconnect? Do you see the problem?

Effective negotiation skills apply across the board. This skill set is one of the most important skill sets you will ever need to learn. Learning how to negotiate not only ensures that you get paid what you're worth, but it also means that you get the respect that you deserve. It also means that people will deal with you like you matter. They will give you the respect that you deserve. They will give you the attention that you've been craving all these years.

That's how important negotiation is and, unfortunately, a lot of people are completely clueless about it. They think that they just need to show up and, somehow, some way, respect is given to them.

I'm telling you respect is not a door prize. In an ideal world, everybody deserves respect and will get respect the moment they show up. However, last time I checked, we do not live in an ideal world. We live in a very chaotic, unfair and, unfortunately, very competitive world. It's very easy for people who are otherwise deserving to fall between the cracks. You might be one of them.

This is why it's really crucial to understand the basics of negotiation and learn in which situations to apply it to and get people to say yes. It really all boils down to becoming a more effective communicator. You have all these hopes, wishes, and needs deep inside you. It really would be sad for you to live the rest of your life thinking you just can't cut it; that, for whatever reason, people are not going to like what you bring to the table.

Their lives might actually be benefited tremendously by what you have to contribute. For that to happen, however, you have to negotiate your place in the table.

You have to be understood, respected, and accepted. Those take negotiation skills.

Take the case of Nelson Mandela. When Nelson Mandela was in prison, the ANC, the African National Congress, his political party, was split up in different factions. Thanks to his negotiation skills, the party reunified.

In fact, Mandela was such a great negotiator that in May of 1990, he went to a crucial meeting with the white majority government. He led a multiracial delegation of ANC members. He didn't make demands. He didn't get into people's faces. Instead, he negotiated by basically talking about the history of the white settlers in South Africa. He looked at their position from their perspective and from a historical point of view.

The other party, and I'm talking about the white minority government representatives, were so impressed by Nelson Mandela's negotiation style that they lifted the state of emergence. This paved the way for the first multi-ethnic elections in South Africa and the rise of the ANC to political power. From there,

Mandela served as the president of South Africa from 1994 to 1999.

It's amazing how much a bit of negotiation skills can take you. Those negotiations could have easily headed south. Things could have easily fallen apart and chaos and open warfare could easily have been the result but now, South Africa has emerged from apartheid as a multiracial society.

Closer to home, my friend Bill learned the importance of honing one's negotiation skills. Keep in mind that negotiation is not part of Bill's job description. Bill was a researcher. There was rarely any interpersonal activity in his work. He is a man of ideas and is more comfortable with books, ideas, and numbers.

Bill was very happy with his work. He kept to himself. He got paid to travel to search materials. He was happy as a clam but there was only one problem. He was getting paid a very miserable wage. Indeed, despite that his company would send him all over the world for research projects, he basically was just getting money to hop from one library or research center after another. Outside of that, there were hardly any extras and when you factor in his take-home pay, he really didn't get paid what he was worth.

Still, his job was so crucial to the company that he was working for that they refused to hire other people. They knew Bill was up to the job. They knew Bill's work was so vital and so important of such a high quality that they didn't need to hire extra personnel. In other words, they looked at my friend Bill as their company asset who was worth at least five people.

I let Bill know about this. When he told me what was going on at the office and what he was doing, I put to him two and two together. I saw the big picture and I told him pointblank, "You are selling yourself short. The company needs you more than you need the company. Keep in mind that you're doing the job of three to five people. Shouldn't you at least be making more? Shouldn't you at least be getting some extras when you travel abroad?"

This blew Bill's mind because he was just focused on his job and, at some level or other, he was just grateful to have the kind of job he had. He was thinking to himself that he was one of the luckiest people in the world because he is actually getting paid to travel all over the world.

That's awesome and everything but you also have to pay for an apartment. You also have to save enough money so you can buy a home later on or make some crucial investments like your retirement. In other words, I made it clear to Bill that he needed to have a game plan for the future and a lot of that game plan has to be funded. In other words, he has to make money... real money.

Bill took my advice to heart and, after a couple of weeks, he brought himself together enough to walk to the company owner's office to ask for a raise. His knuckles were white with fear. He could barely stop sweating but he kept to the script that I told him.

In the meeting, there were three managers present in addition to the owner of the company. Everybody had a fancy title. Everybody knew the position each person held in the company. Bill felt the electricity. In fact, he could have easily felt that they were ganging up on him because they were lined up in a semicircle in front of him, basically hearing him out, but it felt more like an inquisition.

Just as I instructed Bill, he refused to get in people's faces and demand, "Give me what I am worth." Instead, I instructed Bill to say to the crew that he is aware of the value that he is bringing to the team. He also expressed his gratitude for being part of the team but he has to make a living. He has to scale up because compared to other researchers of other companies, Bill wasn't making all that much. I'm happy to report that after that meeting, Bill doubled his salary.

You have to understand that the people who employed Bill are not stupid. They know that the work that he does and the value of his output is easily worth five times what they're paying him. Accordingly, they have a lot of room to move. They doubled his pay. That's mind-blogging to a lot of people but, think about it, they're still generating a decent profit from his work.

This is the whole point of effective negotiation. What Bill did is to make it clear to all the parties involved that there is a win-win situation possible. It doesn't have to be the case where for somebody to win, somebody else has to lose. There is such a thing as both sides getting something and walking away satisfied.

That's precisely what happened because the company won big time by having Bill essentially renew his loyalty and ties to the company because he is now getting paid what he is worth. This means that the company will continue to generate a significant profit based only on the labor of one strategic person like Bill. Bill's happy, the company is happy and the company can continue to scale up and go where it needs to go.

This is the goal of effective negotiation. For one party to win, the other party doesn't have to lose. There is such a thing as a win-win situation. This win-win situation doesn't have to happen now. It doesn't have to be obvious immediately but if everybody can see the big picture and can see that this arrangement that they're getting into or reaffirming is worth hanging onto, then the negotiations would have produced positive results.

You Need to Become a Better Negotiator

If you're reading this book, you are already thinking of taking your negotiation skills to the next level. I congratulate you.

However, if you are still kind of unclear as to why you need to do it or how you're going to do it, let me tell you, you have to be a more skillful negotiator; otherwise, you're not going to get what you have coming to you. That's the bottom line.

This really is all about self-respect. Are you getting the respect that you deserve?

Please understand that there's an open market out there. If the company that you're in doesn't value you like they should, use your negotiation skills to deal with another company that would.

If your significant other continues disrespect you, devalue you, or marginalize or even ignore you, use your negotiation skills to draw a line in the sand in your relationship because, at the end of the day, it's his or her loss, not yours.

If you're having issues with your parents or family members, learn how to negotiate because well-defined boundaries help relationships mature. People may have enough time adjusting to them but, eventually, they will come around and this will make your relationship with your family members so much better.

Stop getting stepped on. Stop getting taken advantage of. Stop getting disrespected to your face. Stop being devaluated. You deserve more.

This book teaches you how to become a skillful negotiator in the business context but you can use these same tips to apply across the board. Whether we're talking about your school, your relationships, your work, your business, or anything else, the information contained in this book will help you take your life to the next level.

Chapter 1: What Makes a Skillful Negotiator Anyway?

Now that you have a clear understanding why you need to become a better negotiator, the next question to ask is what constitutes a skillful negotiator? What complete skill set do you need to have for you to be able to negotiate successfully in most circumstances?

Of course there's no such thing as a perfect negotiator. Everybody could use improvement, even the most experienced and successful negotiators. Still, what follows is a good laundry list of attributes that would make a person a better and more skillful negotiator. Obviously, the more of these traits you have, the better off you would be as far as your negotiation skills go.

You are Willing to Prepare

Skillful negotiators don't just jump in with both feet. They don't wing it. They don't improvise everything on the fly. While a significant amount of improvisation is absolutely necessary because situations change very rapidly, you still have to have a game plan. You still have to have the basics of the specific deal you're trying to get at in your head and must be prepared adequately.

This doesn't mean that you can't stop away from it nor does this mean that you have to completely throw everything in exchange for a "better deal." Instead, when you're prepared, you establish a broad context within which to negotiate so you can scale up the quality of your deals or prepare the least amount that you would be happy with.

Compare this with coming in completely unprepared. Chances are you might give away the farm or you might fail to take advantage of a tremendous opportunity that opens up at the last minute. None of these situations is good. A little preparation goes a long way.

Expect the Best

Skillful negotiators don't come in expecting the worst. They definitely don't come in expecting to lose.

Instead, they expect the best while prepared for the challenges up ahead.

This doesn't mean that they are wearing rose-colored glasses and unrealistically optimistic. No. Great expectations mean that you are pumped up enough and excited enough to work hard for your position to make deals happen.

Everybody knows that perfect deals don't always happen. That's a fact a life but when you come in with high expectations, you align your intellectual preparation with your emotional state and this gives you the push that you need to work as hard as you can towards the best negotiated outcome.

The Patience and Willingness to Learn and Listen

It's very hard to understand the other side of the conversation if you are constantly interrupted. It's very hard to learn from your opponent their perspective of the deal if you can't shut up. Learn to listen to them. Put yourself in their shoes. What's in it for them?

When you put these factors together, you start gaining a tremendous competitive advantage. In many cases, people who start out with a tremendous amount of opposition and negativity are usually just wanting to get hurt. They just want to feel that they matter. They are dragging their heels and putting up a fight oftentimes just because they feel that they're not getting the respect that they deserve.

When you listen to people, you give people respect. This is especially true when you summarize or recap what they just said. They feel that you heard them. They feel that they are important enough to you that you at least listened and put together what they had to say. This opens a gateway for better communications, which can lead to better negotiation outcomes.

Great outcomes are not always guaranteed but, believe me, when you start with great listening, you put yourself on a better footing than just charging in and looking and acting like you don't care about the other side. Believe me they will put up a fight, you will put up a fight, and it's not going to be pretty.

You are Committed to the Highest Level of Personal Integrity

The worst thing that you can do as a negotiator is to lie, misrepresent, or otherwise hide the ball. Please understand that when people think that they're being taken for a ride, they're going to fight for dear life. If you think they've dug in their heels and are putting up quite a fight right now and are being difficult, you've got another thing coming.

People don't like to deal with liars and frauds and scumbags. We all have a built-in defense mechanism against such people. Don't come off like them. Don't give off nonverbal signals that you are trying to pull a fast one. Lay your cards on the table and say, "This is where I'm coming from."

This doesn't mean that you're going to give all your reasons but show you cards. There is a difference. They will respect you more, and this can lead to a better negotiated settlement.

Believe me if you act with the highest level of personal integrity with this negotiation, chances are you will be able to negotiate better deals in the future because people know you're a straight shooter. People know that you're not going to turn around and rip them off or backtrack on what you just said.

People don't have the time for that and if word gets out that you are untrustworthy, it's going to be very hard for you to negotiate in the future. You will almost always find yourself talking to a wall because people put up defenses when they think that they are dealing with somebody who is not a straight shooter.

Communicate Clearly with Persuasion in Mind

A skillful negotiator doesn't just open his or her mouth to empty out his or her thoughts. While that is a necessary first step, it is by no means the whole point of negotiation.

Remember negotiation means persuading the other person to come around to your position or at least split the difference or compromise so you create a win-win situation. This means that you're not just communicating clearly so people can be on the same page as to where you're coming from but you're also communicating so that they would agree with you and would want to cut a deal with you. There is a difference.

You Remember All the Crucial Details

A great negotiator understands that a deal is made up of important details and less important ones. Don't get lost in the weeds.

Lousy negotiators focus on the nickel and dime, nitty-gritty details that at the end of day don't really matter. They fight tooth and nail for those trivial things but they end up losing the big battle.

Focus on and always remember the big picture. What is the outcome that you're looking for? Is it possible to give on certain points and still walk away with the outcome that you desire? If so, then do that.

If you think that negotiation s is somehow a test of your manhood, your personhood, how much the other side respects you, then you're going to get lost in the weeds. You're going to beat each other up over details that eventually don't really matter.

Focus on the big picture. Focus on the outcome that you're looking for. This is how you play the game. To do that, you have to remember the factors that lead to the big outcomes.

Speak Efficiently

A lot of rookie negotiators are confused on this one. They've seen master negotiators in action. They automatically assume that if somebody is articulate and great with words and are very quick speakers that these necessarily translate to great negotiation skills. Absolutely wrong.

You have to make sense. You also have to carry yourself with a high level of integrity. If you're talking very quickly because it seems that you're trying to weasel out of tough situations or essentially just bombard the other side with useless data so you can seal a deal on the sly, you're being deceptive. You're not being upfront. You're using tricks. In other words, you are not operating at a high level of integrity.

This doesn't mean that you have to talk really slow but all this means is that you have to talk clearly. Everybody has to be on the same page. Remember you're trying to create a win-win situation so you can come back to the well again and again and again. Your reputation can reborn from this negotiation.

If people walk away thinking you are a high-quality, top-notch, and trustworthy person who can deliver win-win deals, what do you think they'll do? They'll keep coming back to you. This is a no-brainer.

Why? There are so many scumbags out there. There are so many people who lie through their teeth. There are so many people who hide the ball. There are so many people who agree to a deal and then try to take it back the next day. People are tired of that. They don't have time for that garbage.

So, articulate yourself in a way that emphasizes your integrity. There's no need for quick talk. You're not a used car salesman trying to put one over an unsuspecting customer. You're trying to get a win-win deal.

You must Withstand the Stress

I wish I could tell you that if you just have all the attributes prior to this point that everything will fall into place. Unfortunately, if I were to say that you, I'd be lying. No joke.

You have to understand that, in many cases, the first reaction you would get from the other party is a door to your face. That's right. They'll slam the door and you will get that "no." Most people develop stress during such situations.

Similarly, you can be talking to the other party and they're just going in and out of different issues. They're zigzagging all over the place and, before you know it, after many hours spent and hundreds of dollars blown on lunch, you're still no closer to a deal.

Both of these situations lead to the same place. You're stressed. You're anxious. You might even be depressed.

Great negotiators don't let the stress and the high stakes get the better of them. Instead, they thrive on the stress. They look at it as some sort of gateway experience to a higher level of performance. So what, the deal is going to cost millions of dollars? So what, this is a make-or-break deal for your struggling company? So what, your reputation hangs on the line?

Look at the big picture. Understand that the number one test here is you how you're able to peace things together and you are not going to be doing yourself any favors by falling apart at the last minute. You're definitely not going to be establishing the right reputation when you let stress get the better of you.

Expert negotiators handle high-stakes negotiation cool as a pickle. Why? They can see the big picture. You can too.

Always be Ready to Accept a Compromise

This is a double-barreled factor. For you to accept a compromise, you must first know that there is a compromise possible. This means that you have to have an eye for compromise.

Again, a lot of this has to do with maturity. Inexperienced rookie negotiators who have a chip on their shoulder or who have something to prove rule out the ideal of a compromise. They may not do it consciously but in terms of their assumptions and the way they carry themselves and definitely going by the way they talk, that's what they're doing.

What do you think happens to the other side? You're basically convincing the other side that they have to gun for their negotiated outcome. In other words, they're shooting for their ideal outcome. You're left shooting for yours. What do you think will happen?

I'm not saying that this forecloses on any possibility of a win-win situation but it definitely makes it harder because now you're going to be poles apart. If you come in with a willingness to accept some sort of compromise and you have a good idea of what such a compromise might look like, then you are in a better position because you can push the other side from your point of compromise to their extreme point to somewhere in the middle. This is better than what you would have if you started from the extreme or came off as demanding that they cave to your extreme demands.

Skillful Negotiators have the Air of Flexibility

Pay attention to the heading. I didn't say they are flexible. I didn't say that they are the essence of flexibility. Instead, I said that skillful negotiators have the air of flexibility.

What's the difference? It's all about perception. If people can perceive you as being able to bend or as being able to accommodate to get a better deal, they are more likely to respond to you favorably. This doesn't necessarily mean that you will. This doesn't necessarily mean that you have the tools to do so. As long as you give the impression that you are flexible enough, things can happen.

This is very important because you're not hiding the ball. You're basically just saying, "Okay, I'm ready to work with you but give me something to work with."

Compare this with you coming in for the kill. It's obvious that there's only one thing on your mind. It's obvious that you wish to me at any cost.

Don't expect people to just roll over. It doesn't work that way. They're going to put up a fight. Remember when people are dumbfounded, because you just rushed in with this very inflexible look like you're in for a scorched earth, winner-take-all type of situation, people would put up a fight. In fact, they might even make it a personal mission of theirs to stand up for you because they're trying to prove something to themselves. That is the worst reaction you would want.

Instead, bring the air of flexibility. Come in basically saying, "I'm here to deal. As long as you're open, I'm open. Everything's on the table." Of course, you're going to have to back up your words. You can't say everything's on the table with the intention that basically you're just going to give half of something. That's not going to work. You're going to come off as deceptive, untrustworthy and eventually if you keep it up, people will look at you as a scumbag and they would be very inflexible with you.

Willingness to Search for Compromise

Being able to compromise is one thing and identifying particular areas for compromise is another but readily and eagerly looking for such a compromise will make you stand out. Please understand just because you're looking eagerly for a compromise doesn't mean that the deal will push through. This doesn't mean that you will convince the other side but it does show goodwill. It does show that you're not there to bash people over the head and attack on a winner-take-all basis. At the very least, their "fight or flight" mechanism isn't triggered.

You are Ready to Talk Another Day

When you give the impression that you are ready, if things don't work out, to talk another day, you're basically keeping the lines of communication open. This is very important because negotiations often turn on a dime.

In fact, in many cases, when you're dealing with large organizations or fast-moving smaller organizations, they may not be all that happy with the deal you are proposing. However, before the day is over, there might be certain events or circumstances that happen, which brings them back to the table or at least makes them reopen the conversation again.

This is why it's crucial to keep the lines of communication open. You're not saying, "This is the end. You did not give me the deal that I'm looking for. Forget you. It's over." Don't do that.

Great negotiators always leave things open. They leave it uncertain but they do a good job of clarifying the value proposition they have to offer.

In other words, if you know that the deal is not going to work out, that the other side is simply not going to come around to your position or even to a compromise point, that's fine. However, you recap your position by saying, "This is what I have to offer. This is A, B, C and when that happens, the other side is in a good position to pay close attention to what you're lining up, what you're listing.

This reminds them of why they're negotiating with you in the first place. This is the top of mind to them. So, when they go back to the office or they go home and other pressing circumstances happen, they realize that they have to pay bills, they realize that another company is trying to make a move on your company or a similar company, who knows what the other factors are.

However, once they realize those and they remember your value proposition and the fact that lines of communication are still open, don't be surprised if they're ready to deal. In fact, it normally happens that when negotiations reach an impasse, the next day a great deal happens. This is only possible if you keep your lines of communication open.

If Other People Can Do It, You Can Do It

I know you've heard that saying before. If other people can do it, I can do it too. It's a nice pep talk. It's a nice little self-help tagline but, believe me, it's absolutely true.

You have to remember that great negotiators are usually not born. I'm not going to lie to you and say that there are a certain percentage of people who are just born with a silver tongue. They know how to say the right things at the right time with the right people to produce the right outcomes over and over again. Those people do exist but they are few and far between.

For the vast majority of successful negotiators out there, they learned their craft. They weren't born that way. How do you learn? You try, you fail. You try, you fail again. You try until you achieve a breakthrough and then you try again and fail and you repeat the process over and over again.

If they can do it, you can do it too. You just need to go through that process. This has less to with skill and more to do with attitude. You have to understand that aptitude, meaning the ability to get certain things done a certain way to produce certain outcomes follows attitude.

If you're ready, willing, and eager to learn, you will learn even if you are punching above your weight. Maybe it will take your several repetitions. Perhaps you will get knocked down a lot more times before everything starts to line up but you'll get there. You just have to want to do it.

On the other hand, if you don't want to do it, then it doesn't matter whether you are some sort of super genius. It doesn't really matter that you are able to hear instructions once and know perfectly well what to do. None of that would matter because you don't have the attitude to pick up the right aptitude.

None of this is going to happen overnight. This takes experimentation. This takes challenging yourself. This takes patience.

Are you ready to take the journey? Are you ready to become a great negotiator? You have to commit to this. You can't just say, "Yes, I'm ready" and forget about it. When you say yes, you have to mean it. You have to dedicate yourself to this because it's going to take time and patience.

Other Myths about Negotiation

I have already killed one myth (I hope I did in your mind): Great negotiators are born, not made.

Unfortunately, there are many other common misconceptions and myths about expert negotiation. You have to disabuse yourself for this if you want to have any shot at becoming good at negotiations.

Negotiations are All about Winning or Losing

Drop the black-and-white conception of negotiation. Believe it or not, there are deals that are gray in nature. Both parties are not perfectly thrilled with the deal that they have but they'll make do with it. It's at least marginally better than what they started with. Believe it or not, a significant percentage of all negotiations end up with gray, not black or white.

Unfortunately, if you come in with the attitude and the misconception that negotiation must either produce a clear winner or a clear loser, then you're just making things harder on yourself. You probably will end up triggering that flight-or-fight mindset on the opposing side.

What do you think they will do? That's right. They'll dig in their heels and put up a fight because, all of a sudden, this is about their pride. They don't want to look bad. Before you know it, you've given them some sort of motivation to prove something to themselves. You'll continue to hear the word "no."

You have to Always Take the Initiative with the First Offer

Another misconception about being a good negotiator is to always make the first move as far as offers go. In the words, if you're trying to get a good deal on the house, low-ball the seller. After all, you're being ambitious; your boldness is evident; and people can see that you may mean business although you came in with a low-ball offer.

This is going to backfire because you did not take the time to look at the other side's perspective. At the very least, you did not appear to be taking their perspective. More likely than not, they're going to put a up fight or they won't take you seriously at all.

You don't have to make the first offer. You can talk to them and communicate your desire about the property or the deal and then they can make the first move.

It's actually better when they do that because it shows their hand. Maybe they've been sitting on the property or the company for five years and it's bleeding them dry. Maybe they have a hot potato on their hands and they'd rather just unload. While they did put a price tag, on their property, please keep in mind that this is just a starting point. That's the whole point of negotiation. Everything is just a starting point.

You can be Nice and Still Win in Negotiations

A very common and stubborn misconception about negotiation skills involves the issue of niceness. For the largest time, it's very easy for people to think that if you are nice, easy to get along with, easy to understand, and talks at a modern rate that you are somehow a pushover. A lot of rookie negotiators even think that you are setting yourself up for failure.

This is not true. Nice people tend to make friends. People would want to come back to the negotiation table with you on another deal. How come? They see that you are pleasant. They see that you're open. They see that you work with a high level of integrity. Who wouldn't want to work with a person like that?

Who would you rather have? Somebody who is sneaky, stabs you in the back, lies through his teeth, and works at an unfair advantage at each and every time? Most people are toxic. You can't wait to finish negotiating with them so you can get them out of your life. The sooner the better.

It is no surprise that people who resort to dirty tricks in negotiation can win from time to time but guess what? They cannot win their victories. They're always looking for new victims and before they know it, word gets out about their character that people just stonewall them. In other words, people just don't want to deal with them. You don't want to be that guy. So, be nice.

This doesn't mean that you have to go out of your way. This doesn't mean that you have to go out on a limb and basically pull out your arm for the other side to take advantage of you but be nice. Be upfront. Be cleared with your agenda.

The moment smell that you're trying to pull a fast one is the moment that you make things unnecessarily harder on yourself.

Keep the information above in mind as you start learning the craft of expert negotiations. Understand these factors because when we get to Chapter 4 and walk you through the specific negotiation tactics that you're going to use, these factors are going to be in play.

Chapter 2: Why Negotiation Skills Are So Important?

If I haven't made it clear already in the introduction of this book, negotiations are crucial to your success. Period. Whether you want to advance your career, become a better or more persuasive communicator or would like to become a better leader, you need to know how to negotiate.

On a personal level, if you don't want people to step all over your or take advantage of you, you also need this skill. In fact, if you are dealing with any other human being on this planet, negotiations will invariably enter the picture.

Obviously, in most situations, you have to ask for something from somebody. They might be charging a higher price. They might not even want to give it to you. Regardless of what it is, when you know how to negotiate, you make things easier for yourself.

This doesn't necessarily mean you always walk away with the best deals. But this does mean that people will respect you. People will understand that you know how to get around and they are less likely to take advantage of you.

It also helps in building up your reputation. Regardless of how you cut it, when you know how to negotiate, you become a more effective person. If you have any kind of goals that you've set for yourself, you would have to negotiate.

Either you need deals or you need to get into opportunities. It doesn't really matter. Negotiation skills will always be required. At the end of the day, being a good negotiator goes hand in hand with being great at relationships.

If you want to build, maintain and improve or repair relationships, you have to know how to negotiate. This means that you have to learn how to effectively communicate your desires in such a way that people will not only understand it clearly, but go along with you.

It takes a long time to become a great negotiator and this training process pushes you to be more persistent, persevering and deficient.

Finally, if you want to be a peacemaker or you would like to keep the peace in all your relationships, being a great negotiator enables you to eliminate friction. People being people, there will always be areas for friction. We don't always see eye to eye. There are always loose ends and details that threaten smooth relationships.

Small misconceptions and misunderstandings can easily get blown out of proportion and things can get out of hand. It takes both a cool head and solid negotiation skills to maintain harmonious relationships.

If you're not doing it for yourself, do it for other around you.

If negotiation skills are so important, why do most people have a hard time with it?

Most people didn't bother to learn how to negotiate

The main reason why a lot of people have a tough time negotiating is because they didn't get around to learning it in a formal way. They didn't sit down and ask themselves, "Okay, what am I going to do? Oh! I'm going to negotiate. This is what I need to do."

They didn't think that far ahead. A lot of people are under the impression that they already have this built in ability to negotiate. This is a very common mistake and that's why people almost always don't get the best deal possible. Expert negotiators allowed themselves to learn how to negotiate. Seems pretty basic but most people don't get it.

Their parents don't usually teach children how to negotiate

When you're dealing with a parent, it's usually their way or the high way. You are usually handed a command on a purely take it or leave it basis. It is no surprise that when parent approach their children that way and position the relationship along those lines, kids don't learn how to negotiate.

Please understand that a large chunk of what makes you a functional person comes from your parents. Your parents are the initial source of your training as a human being. If negotiation skills are not part of that initial training, then don't be surprised if you have a tough time negotiating.

A lot of parents nowadays are pushing their kids to think and negotiate terms. But this is a fairly recent development. For the longest time, when you are dealing with a parent, they always say that this is the right way to do it or you're better off not doing it at all.

They either spoon feed you or they just give you black and white choices. There's little space for negotiation between these 2 options.

We are not taught to negotiate in school

If you thought your relationship with your parents involves some sort of top down hierarchical "do what I say" type of relationship, the typical school takes this model to a whole other level.

When you go to a traditional school, you are basically given a curriculum, a set schedule and a well defined way of doing things. You either go along with that process or there's going to be a problem.

There is no space for negotiation. There is no space for open ended questioning that can lead to negotiated solutions. Again, it's a take it or leave it kind of package. It is no surprise that given this institutional setting, kids don't know how to negotiate because as far as the school is concerned, there's nothing to negotiate.

It isn't offered as a formal course or class. It is not incorporated in the curriculum.

We simply don't believe that negotiation can be taught

Finally, one of the main reasons why people have a hard time negotiating is they simply don't believe that this type of thing can be taught. They don't believe that you can open a book and learn the basics of negotiation and through hard work, practice and discipline over an extended period of time, become a master negotiator.

Again, we go back to that common myth that great negotiators are born. They are not made. Well, the opposite is true. The vast majority of expert negotiators out there weren't born that way.

In fact, a lot of them, at first, couldn't negotiate themselves out of a wet paper bag. But through patience, perseverance and continues training, they are at the top of their game. If they can do it, you can do it too provided you have the right tools. This book is one of the tools you need to become a master negotiator.

In the following chapter, I'm going to give you an overview of 7 strategies that will help you master negotiation. Starting with chapter 4, I'm going to spell out what these strategies are so you can apply them to your daily life.

The key here is practice. Make no mistake. If you can see the opportunities to negotiate all around you, you will be able to become a master negotiator. You will give yourself the opportunity to try and hone these strategies until you put together something that works for you.

Please understand that these 7 strategies are not to be interpreted as some sort of cookie cutter, one size fits all solution that applies to all people at all times. That's not the intention behind these strategies.

Instead, they are intended to help you create a framework that works best in your particular set of circumstances. You have to tweak them. You have to apply them to the situation on the ground as far as your present everyday life is concerned.

Then and only then would you be able to benefit fully from them so that all these materials will apply to your daily life on a cumulative basis. In other words, it becomes harder and harder for you to forget what you learned in the past and your overall knowledge about negotiation, when to use it, who to use it on, what kind of outcome to shoot for and all that other good stuff builds up in value over time.

That's the proper way of using the information you get from this book. Don't look at it as some sort of magical check list that you just need to follow and all of a sudden, you become a master negotiator. It doesn't work that way.

Chapter 3: 7 Sure-Fire Strategies To Master Negotiation

This is a quick breakdown of all the following chapters. I've listed the 7 strategies below and starting with chapter 4, I will discuss in detail each of these strategies

Strategy #1: Strengthen your bargaining power

You have to have something to offer. You have to have something of value to begin with because your counterparts perception of your starting hand plays a big role in how they shape their negotiating position. If they feel that you have very little to offer, expect stiff resistance.

On the other hand, if you have a very compelling starting hand, don't be surprised if they come off as initially more accommodating.

Strategy #2: Set the logistics

Taking the initiative to coordinate how you're going to meet, where you're going to meet, when you're going to meet and other crucial terms enables you to pre-qualify the other party.

They can see that you're in command. They can see that you're serious. This can go a long way in securing a more favorable deal out of your negotiations.

Strategy #3: Focus on building rapport

Make sure you establish mutual comfort. This leads to you seeing eye to eye and establishing the fact that you're not necessarily in the same room to beat each other up or to gain an unfair advantage over each other.

This takes the adversarial air out of the negotiations and enables people to drill down to the stuff that really matters instead of wasting precious energy and time on brinksmanship.

Strategy #4: Be in the right mood

You can't have a poker face during negotiations. You have to have the right emotions on your face because your emotions influence the final resolution of the negotiation.

Strategy #5: Be the first to make the offer
When you take the initiative in making the offer, you set the tone and the range of the negotiation. The negotiation starts to work around the first move you made. This gives you the upper hand.

Strategy #6: Frame a win win offer

Make sure you package or position your offer in such a way that it's obvious that the other side and your party will win from your offer. Do not position it as a "I win, you lose" offer. This makes the offer more palatable and easier to live with to the other party.

Strategy #7: Be ready to counter their offer

The worst thing you can do is to get caught flat footed when the other side makes a counter offer to your offer. It may be a very generous offer, or at least seem like it. These are the most dangerous.

It makes you think that they've given in. It turns out you probably would've gotten a much better deal. So get ready to counter their offer, whatever it is.

Chapter 4: Anyone Can Learn Superior Bargaining Power

You have to strengthen your bargaining power prior to negotiations. This is a powerful way of pre-qualifying the other party. If they are under the impression that you really don't have much to offer or the value that you are seeking to offer is not really all that high, don't be surprised that they low ball you.

It wouldn't be too shocking if they put up a wall because in their head, you don't really have much to offer. Either they can get it from somewhere else or the intrinsic value of what you have to offer really isn't that compelling.

Sure, they might not be able to get it readily from elsewhere, but they're not necessarily in a rush to do a deal with you either. That's how low they view your bargaining power.

Great negotiators do a good job selling the other side first before they negotiate. One way to do this is to say,

"This deal is a miracle because I've got 5 other people lining up for this property. They need it immediately and despite my busy schedule, I decided to call you and see what you think. I know that you are interested in this property as well. So I figured in fairness because you approached me first to hear your offer."

Pay attention to what I just said. Do you see the value that you put in your offer? Do you see how you position whatever it is you're selling or whatever it is you possess in the eyes of the other party?

The key here is value. Put more precisely, we're talking about perceived value. You see, when it comes to negotiations, perception is reality. Little do they know the 5 people that spoke to you about the property may not be all that excited about the property. They just want to price out the neighborhood.

Maybe they are interested, but they're not ready to buy right now. Whatever the case may be, you don't have to mention those details. You just have to say, "I was approached by several people about this property."

The key is to control the perception of value. When you say those things, what do you trigger? That's right. You trigger the all too human fear of scarcity. Thousands of years ago, our ancestors were walking through savannas. These are grass lands in Africa.

They didn't know where their next meal is going to come from. So when they see a game animal, maybe it's a wildebeest, or some sort of buffalo or zebra, they kill it because they know that the next time they eat may be days, if not weeks, from now.

This scarcity mindset has been seared into the human DNA. No matter how cool the negotiator across the table from your may appear, he or she will have that scarcity DNA. When you say, "There are lots of people who are interested in this property, but I'm talking to you first" you trigger that.

A variation of this is "I just got through a job interview with your biggest competitor and I just wanted to interview with you because I'd like to know more about your company." Again, you're triggering the scarcity mindset because at the back of their heads, they're thinking, "I better jump on this now because somebody else might get it."

This mindset is not so much different from an early cave man thinking, "I better eat this game animal now otherwise it'll be gone tomorrow. Who knows when I'll eat next?" Do you see the power of qualification? You have to come off with a perception of value.

Tap the power of BATNA

One way that you can enhance your bargaining power is to play up your BATNA, also known as best alternative to a negotiated agreement. Before you negotiate, you have to research the other options available to you just in case your upcoming negotiation falls apart.

Not only will this give you other options and make you feel more confident coming into the negotiations, but it also gives you facts to share with your counterpart. When you're exploring your BATNA, you may run into alternative offers.

You may get other valuations. You may see other opportunities. This is very important on both a subjective basis (what's going on in your head and your moods) as well as on an objective basis.

On an objective basis, when you explore your BATNA, you end up appraising the value of the asset or the resource you're negotiating over. This means that you know what you're representing and what you're standing on which in turn, pumps up your motivation to negotiate for its full value.

There's this strong interplay between objective validation and subjective encouragement. When you come in, you don't give out the perception that you have a weak card. You know the value of what you bring to the table and your counterpart can sense your confidence.

This is how BATNAs enhance your bargaining power. It is a form of pre-qualification. In a study published in a journal of applied psychology in April 2005, researchers measured the impact of BATNA to contribution when it comes to negotiator performance.

Contribution is when one party value the negotiation based on what they can add to the deal. They look at what they can contribute.

In the study of 140 business school graduate students, participants were asked how they would like to distribute profits and what would be acceptable to them. It turns out that the graduate students who were assigned greater BATNA are quite impressive when negotiations begin.

This is due to the fact that BATNA tends to pre-qualify participants before negotiations really proceed. But interestingly enough, as the negotiations proceed because of areas for bargaining like negotiating a profit distribution as well as who will do what, the more people are able to bargain the weaker inherently superior BATNA become.

This study highlights the point that people have strong initial bargaining power thanks to BATNA. They shouldn't be too quick to bargain so as to diminish their initial strong hand. In other words, if you're going to come into a negotiation, emphasize the strength of your position.

Emphasize your BATNA. This would then qualify the other side so you can get to a better deal. Otherwise, if you just go straight to negotiation and you just downplay the BATNA that you have, don't be surprised if you end up with a less than optimal deal.

The key takeaway here is to be as transparent with your BATNA as possible. Make it shine. This will let the other party know that you bring a good deal. So they better step up with their best deal.

Similarly, in a 2009 study in the journal of applied psychology, 198 volunteers were observed to determine the relationship between how straightforward negotiators are and their concessions they're likely to make.

The study participants were initially asked to fill out a questionnaire which measured how straightforward they were and also paid attention to certain personality traits that they may have.

After they have filled out the questionnaires, they would then be assigned to different role playing groups and each was given a room. One role playing group is the pinnacle and the other is the mountain.

These different groups were then asked to represent either the pinnacle or the mountain company and they're supposed to negotiate with each other to come to an agreement regarding 7 issues involving how much money employees would be paid as well as the management of human resources.

The different pairings were given up to 45 minutes to negotiate on the 7 issues. The outcomes of the negotiations are then recorded. Researchers then cross reference the negotiated outcomes with the personality profiles of the participants.

The research concluded that there is a high correlation between straightforwardness and the ability to concede as well as to look out for the needs of the other party. In other words, if you're straightforward, you're more likely to get concessions from the other side than if you were playing it sly or you're trying to hid your agenda.

The researchers believe that this is due to the fact that straightforwardness is an individual trait that influences the behavior of the other party in the negotiations. If they perceive you as a straight shooter, they're more likely to concede in exchange for a concession from you in the hopes of getting a win win situation.

On the other hand, if they don't see you as straightforward, they're less likely to give an inch.

Step by step process for strengthening your initial bargaining power

Step #1: Identify and improve your BATNA

The first thing you need to do is look at what your best alternative is to a negotiated agreement with the other party. Is it strong? Is it weak? Is it negligible? What can you do to improve it? Can you find a better buyer? Can you combine it with another service that you offer to come up with a better value proposition that other people would find compelling?

If you're looking for a job, are there better job offers in this industry or another industry? This takes quite a bit of research. You have to be clear as to what your BATNA is because believe me, the other party will not do it for you.

Instead, they will grind you down and say, "Well you don't really have much to offer. So we'll low ball you." Don't let that happen by being clear as to what your BATNA is and work hard to improve it.

By improving, it really all boils down to positioning. You may have a profoundly weak product. But that's not a death sentence in of itself. You can package it or bundle it with other products. You can partner with others. You can get a review. There's so many things you can do to appear less weak.

Step #2: Identify and zero in on your counterpart's BATNA

If you have a BATNA, the other side has a BATNA as well. You have to do your research here. They're not going to tell you. Maybe the reason why they want to buy your company is because they want to sell the combined company later.

That would be a great piece of information to know coming into negotiations. Similarly, their company might be going under. So they need your company as some sort of life support.

They may have the cash, but they know that the handwriting is on the wall as far as their company's product maturity or service life trajectory go. Whatever the case may be, their large scale operation has a limited life of high profitability. So they're exploring their options.

Knowing this enables you to reposition your BATNA. Don't be afraid to ask questions at this point. Ask people within the organization, ask people in the industry, do your research, get white papers, get research reports, request annual reports or public filings.

Whatever the case may be, do your research. There's a reason why they're talking to you. And often times, it's not because you're weak and they're strong. They need you. That's why they're talking to you. Otherwise, they probably wouldn't be talking to you right here, right now.

Step #3: Show the other party's BATNA in the worst light possible

After you've done your research about the other party's motivations as well as their options, show them your perception of their position in the worst light possible without being insulting.

For example, if you're a manufacturer and your negotiation with an importer with a domestic supplier of raw materials, they can tell you that they are the best domestic producer of the raw material you're looking for.

They will tell you that the material they provide is crucial to your product. Your product simply won't be as good without their raw materials. Fair enough. But you then tell them that you can easily import raw material of the same or superior quality from China at half the price.

When you do this, you just effectively destroyed their BATNA. They're not as confident anymore. In fact, you send them into a tail spin and they are more likely to re-evaluate the value that they bring to the table and this can play into your hands.

You can say, "Well, I can do that. But if get a good deal with you, I'll stick with the domestic producer because I'd like to stay away from importing and just go with domestic production because it's faster and more efficient." You probably already know the reasons to give them.

The key here is to weaken the other party's BATNA so they're not as confident. Which prepares you for the next step.

Step #4: Deliver a firm and confident request

Right after you weaken the other party's BATNA and you play up your BATNA, you then deliver your request. The key here is to not crush the other side. If it's obvious that you're basically just low balling and you're just being unreasonable, you make it easy for them to step away.

You basically would say, "This person is just low balled us. This is not even in the ball park." So, either you're not serious or you're playing games. That's all they need to step out.

There is a fine line between showing dominance, which means you know that they know you have the upper hand. That's why your offer looks like the way it does. This is very different from just being mean, being abusive and just being obnoxious. Know the difference.

Because when you're dominant, you can position the deal closer to your target price or target outcome. On the other hand, if you're perceived as being obnoxious, you don't get a deal at all.

You're not being dominant when you walk away with empty hands because you overplayed your hand. The worst thing that you can do is then to come back to the negotiating table with your tail between your legs. That doesn't do you any favors.

So don't overplay your hand. It's one thing to show dominance. It's another to just be completely obnoxious.

Chapter 5: How to Control the Terms of Any Negotiation

When you take the initiative to dictate, or at least "strongly suggest" how the meeting will happen, where it will take place, and the time and date, you have tremendous control. You come in looking strong.

Remember, as I have mentioned at least a few times previously in this book, negotiation is primarily about perception. Does the other side think you have a strong hand? Are they under the impression that you believe you have the stronger hand and you have a lot more value to offer? Can you give them the impression that they need you more than you need them?

While a lot of this turns on your BATNA, you can help things along as far as building perceptions go by controlling the logistics. If anything, when you try to call the shots regarding how negotiation will happen and other details, you get to feel out the other side.

If they think that they have a losing hand or the negotiations are not as important to them but they still want to do it, they would be more accommodating. They would just go along with what you have in mind and show up.

On the other hand, if they feel that they have a strong hand or if they want to put up a fight, they will let you know. If anything, trying to control the logistics enables you to diagnose or feel out the other side.

Of course, this is not dispositive. Maybe in the beginning they seem so easy, but when it comes to negotiations, they fight you tooth and nail. That happens. But this is usually a good indication.

So, the key here is not to overplay your hand. What you're trying to do is you're trying to create an impression of strength, authority, and confidence.

In other words, you're trying to create a perception that will prequalify the other side to see things from your perspective. This increases the chances that you will get what you came for.

Timing is Crucial to Negotiations

Believe it or not, the way you time the negotiations has an impact on its quality. Usually, when meetings are scheduled later in the day, people are already tired. People have already expended their willpower.

What do you think will happen? Well, they're less likely to deal. Because as the old saying goes, when it doubt, leave things out.

You can't commit when you are unsure about your willpower. Maybe there's a detail that you overlooked, or maybe you haven't fully studied the deal closely enough. Whatever the case may be, if you are sensible and you're a normal person, you would rather put things off instead of painting yourself in a corner. That's how most people deal with late negotiations.

If possible, schedule the negotiation early in the morning. Maybe right when business opens or an hour or two before lunch. Once people go to lunch, all bets are off.

The further away after lunch your negotiation time is, the less likely you would get a firm answer from the other side. Even if they think that they've arrived at a decision, they would still wait until the next day.

Why Does Calling the Shots Make Such a Powerful Impact?

When you set the terms of the negotiations in terms of logistics, you are more likely to get accommodations or concessions from the other side. This is called a "primacy effect."

In a classic analysis done by Benet Murdock in 1962 in the *Journal of Experimental Psychology*, people who are given initial suggestions are more likely to hang on to those suggestions. They have primacy in their minds.

This is explained by Murdock as involving a process where the first things people notice are more likely to be stored effectively in their memories. The thinking is, when an item is stored first, it's easier to remember that item because when any subsequent item is added to memory, the mind goes through a longer process each and every time.

For example, you remember an item and then you rehearse it sub-vocally. Then you try to remember another item, so you first remember the first item, and then the second item, and then you try to remember a third item.

The more items you add on to your memory, the more your brain gets tired. At the end of it all, you're more likely to hang on to the first item because that's the one that keeps getting rehearsed over and over again as you add new entries to long term storage.

This means that, over time, the latter items that you added will decline in recall, but you are more likely to hang on to items earlier in the sequence.

The same applies to primacy when negotiating. When you make the first move and you make key points in the negotiation, these are more likely to be remembered. These are more likely to be the focal points of subsequent negotiations.

In other words, you set the agenda. And being able to set the terms also sends the signal of authority.

Another key variation of this strategy is to take the initiative in terms of weather. When setting up logistics, try to set up negotiations when it's sunny out.

When the weather is pleasant, you're more likely to get a better deal from the other side, and you're more likely to be more accommodating. In other words, it's easier to see the win-win situation in the deal.

This link between nice weather and the other party being more helpful, or your side being more helpful, is supported by a research published in March 2013 in the *Journal of Psychology*. In this study, sunshine weather conditions are said to improve mood among people and lead to more positive social relationships.

The study showed pairings of male and female confederates dropping a glove on a sidewalk around subjects who are being studied. The confederate or the assistant of the people running the study would drop a glove unaware he or she dropped it.

Two factors were being tested by the study whether it's sunny or cloudy. The study wasn't done when it was raining. And it turned out that on sunnier days, people are more likely to be helpful. People are more likely to pick up the glove and give it to the person who dropped it.

The study shows that there's a link between external climate, positive moods, and the willingness of people to be helpful. This has a very strong impact on negotiations.

If people in the negotiating party can see outside the window and they see that it's nice, they're more likely to be open. They're more likely to be helpful and less likely to put up a fight unreasonably or ask for unreasonable terms.

Finally, it's also very important to ask for face to face negotiations. If you are negotiating via email, it's very easy for people to just assume a "take it or leave it" approach.

How come? Well, if you're selling online services, the other party can easily comparison shop your services.

They can look for lists of service providers. They have so many other options available to them, thanks to the internet.

This is why it's normally not a good idea to do things via email if you're trying to close a deal. The better approach would be face to face.

Now, even if you're never going to see each other physically face to face, you can still Skype. You can still use Google Hangouts.

The great thing about face to face negotiations is that even though the other side can still use comparison shopping to find alternative services to yours or alternative products, that eye to eye contact is made. It has become personal.

There's that added personal element that leads to a higher level of trust and a sense that they know you, which leads to a higher chance that you will close the deal.

Just how important is eye to eye contact? In a Dutch study released in January 2009, published in the

Journal of Experimental Social Psychology, researchers found that when they observed male and female students negotiating with each other, eye contact plays a big role in sealing a deal.

However, they noticed that there is a distinct difference between males and females. With males, you should reduce nonverbal cues. Basically, you should try to use the phone or negotiate via email, in addition to face to face negotiations.

Ideally, males work better with less face to face contact. For females, this is completely opposite. Maintain eye contact for optimal effect.

Step by Step Instructions for Control and Logistics

Step #1: When planning to negotiate, always select the earlier time

This will help you create a stronger impression.

Step #2: Try to choose great weather when negotiating

As much as you can, try to get weather forecasts for the week that you intend to negotiate. Pick a date that is most likely to have great weather. Negotiate on that day. People are more likely to be helpful when it's pleasant out.

Step #3: Choose the right medium to negotiate

There is a slight difference between males and females when it comes to negotiation medium. For men, it's perfectly acceptable to negotiate via email or phone, with less emphasis on face to face communication. On the other hand, if you're dealing with females, you need to make eye contact and it's good to do video conferencing.

Step #4: Take the initiative to control all logistics

This means that you take the initiative to select all logistical questions. This means choosing your office to negotiate.

This is very important because when you control the premises, the other side is in your territory. They can see what's going on. They can see what you have to offer. They can see what your business is about, so this has a cumulative effect on their perception of you and the value you bring to the table.

Step #5: Always be prepared for a follow-up meeting

While it would be great to conclude all negotiations in one day, oftentimes, this doesn't happen. Do yourself a big favor and prepare for the possibility that things will carry over to another day so make sure that you have enough padding in your schedule to make this happen. A little bit of preparation can go a long way.

Chapter 6: Establish Mutual Comfort To Win Big

There's a common misconception about effective negotiation: you have to intimidate the other party.

While that kind of tactic may look good on movie screens, believe me, in the real world, that's not a very productive strategy. In fact, in most cases, you end up making your job harder than it already is.

You have to understand that people do not like to be taken advantage of. People don't like being made to feel that you are taking something that they have. They will fight you. They will put up a struggle. This is why it's really important to go back to what negotiations really are.

Negotiations are all about effective communication. They have something, you have something, and you're looking for some sort of mutually beneficial exchange.

That's really the heart of negotiations. You're just talking about how to split the difference, what details are involved so you can get what you want and the other party can get what they want.

Of course, there's no such thing as a perfect deal. It's not like you can walk into a negotiation and then walk out with everything that you've asked for and then some. It usually doesn't work that way. In fact, in the vast majority of cases, it doesn't work that way at all.

There's always a give and take. And oftentimes, it doesn't involve the kinds of things that you explicitly asked for.

I raise this issue because it's very easy to think that the more adversarial you are to the other side, that they somehow, will get the message that you are serious.

Once they get the message, according to this mistaken thinking, they will size up their options and are more likely to give you what you're looking for. After all, you're serious. You're dedicated. You're driven.

Well, you can't intimidate your way to a good deal.

Effective deals are all about clearly communicating to the other side what they stand to gain. Once you make that clear, then you reiterate what you're looking for and how that fits into that narrative. That's how you get a good deal going.

And it's crucial that both sides are comfortable. This is why effective negotiators, they come in and they break the ice. They don't come in and give people an icy stare.

They don't look at people down their nose. They don't stand erect with their arms crossed and ready to do battle. They don't do any of that. Expert negotiators often look like meek lambs.

Now, it's very easy to be skeptical and cynical about this kind of thing and say, "Well, that person is actually a wolf dressed in lamb's clothing."

Not necessarily. Remember, the more straightforward you are, and the more trustworthy you appear, the more likely you will get concessions. But a lot of this turns on your ability to give concessions on your end as well.

For this to happen, both sides have to be comfortable. So instead of playing games, work on building rapport by establishing mutual comfort.

In a 2002 study published in the journal *Group Dynamics Theory Research and Practice*, when people "schmooze," they're more likely to get better deals. Please understand that this schmoozing doesn't take place in face to face negotiations, but through email negotiations.

A total of 100 student participants were evenly and randomly assigned the roles of buyers and sellers. They were given information packages and instructions and guidelines. They were asked to follow the guidelines.

Some students were asked to schmooze, meaning, basically get to know the other party through telephone conversations before negotiation. The other group wasn't instructed to schmooze but to get down to business.

When reviewing the results of the negotiations, it turns out that the group that were instructed to schmooze reached an agreement with the other party in 59% of cases. On the other hand, the non-schmoozing group only got a deal going in 40% of cases.

Besides schmoozing and breaking the ice, another way you can get a smooth start to negotiations going is to say something about yourself that is unrelated. It's a form of personal revelation. It can be small. It doesn't have to be big and dramatic.

But when you do this, you become more than a face in the crowd. You're not just another number. You have gone from becoming just another sales quota to an actual flesh and blood human being that they are doing business with. In other words, you end up humanizing yourself, and this has an impact on the results of negotiations.

In a January 1999 study published in the journal *Organizational Behavior and Human Decision Processes*, 194 student participants were given instructions to engage in two-party negotiations strictly through email.

One group was asked to disclose certain personal information, and the other group had no information disclosed to them.

Both groups broke the ice. Basically, they were schmoozing with each other. But it turns out that the group that was instructed to disclose a little bit of themselves secured better deals. The whole negotiation process was less aggressive than the other party.

All of this, of course, revolved around email negotiations.

Another great strategy for establishing mutual comfort is to mirror the other party's behavior.

Why does this work? Well, we like people who are like us. We like people who look like us, talk like us, or have some sort of mannerisms like us. We also like people who are interested in the things that we are interested in.

In a Stanford study published in March of 2008, study participants who were instructed to mimic the people they're negotiating with not only got better deals, but they also tended to increase the overall value of the deal for everyone involved.

In fact, the pairings of study participants where one partner is involved in mimicking or mirroring performed so much better than pairings that did not have a mimicking partner.

Step by Step Guide to Establishing Mutual Comfort and Negotiations

Step #1: Introduce yourself

The first thing that you need to do is to introduce yourself. Now, this goes beyond just saying your name. You also have to say something about yourself. You also have to say something a little bit about your background.

When you do this, you establish common ground. At the very least, you're not just this random person.

You're not a complete and total stranger because you said something personal.

Step #2: Establish eye contact

When you are involved in direct negotiations, establish eye contact when you're introducing yourself. This shows sincerity.

You're telling people around you, in no uncertain terms, that you're not hiding anything. You're being upfront. This is a good way to establish mutual comfort.

Of course, every time you talk, you can't just stare at people straight in the eye, especially men. So once negotiation starts, focus less on eye contact and focus more on nonverbal signals. When negotiating with women, on the other hand, focus on eye contact.

Step #3: Compliment people

As long as you're sincere and authentic, your compliment will break the ice. You're stepping out of bounds. You are offering something free. You are being solicitous.

So, usually, this triggers the human natural response of reciprocity. Generally speaking, when people are good to us, we try to repay the favor. So, when you give a sincere compliment, people will see your good intentions.

But the key is sincerity. You can't be fake. You can't be exaggerated or blown out of proportion.

Step #4: Pay close attention to how they communicate

If you notice that they tend to be verbal people, meaning they tend to nod and don't say much, or they click on pens and they're trying to hear something, pick up on that because you're going to mimic them in Step #5.

If, on the other hand, they say, "I see that," "I see where you're coming from." or "I feel you," take note of that as well.

Different people have different listening styles. Some people are verbal listeners. Meaning, they pay more attention to words and less on eye contact. Other people are very visual.

Finally, other people are tactile. Meaning, they like to hug, they like to focus on how they feel.

So please understand that there's no right or wrong answer. Just make sure that you're locked into the type of communicator you are dealing with.

Step #5: Show interest by mimicking

When you mimic, you're basically locking into their frequency. You're showing them that you get them in a nonverbal and in a low key way.

The key here is low key. Because if it's obvious that you are mirroring somebody, you can easily cross the line between mimicking and mocking. There is a big difference, so watch yourself.

Chapter 7: How Right Mood During Negotiations Does All Magic

When you negotiate, you're communicating on many different levels. There are, of course, the words coming out of your mouth. But when you look at what's going on, verbal communication is a small piece of the puzzle. You have to look at the big picture.

Emotions, emotional intensity, facial expressions, your speaking pace, your gestures, your body language, your posture – all of these and many others form the overall context of your mood.

While it's good to be in a positive mood, it is not absolutely necessary. What's important is that you are communicating acceptance, cordiality, warmth, and openness.

In other words, you're not there to pick up a fight. You're not there to intimidate the other side. You're not giving off these signals that basically say, "Take my deal" or "Give me a great deal or I'll bite your head off." None of that works.

Instead, be in the right mood, which basically invites agreement. You're basically saying, "I'm here to deal. I'm here in good faith and I'm here to give you what you want while I expect to get what I want."

It's important to make sure that you show no visual signs of fearing disappointment, stress or anxiety about an unforeseen result. In other worlds, people aren't turned on by worry.

When you go into a negotiation, the other party is not going to be excited if you look like you're guilty, disappointed, letdown, sad, or stressed out because that's going to stress them out as well.

So, check yourself by looking in the mirror. Are you communicating clearly with all your verbal and nonverbal communication assets what you're feeling deep down inside? Make sure it lines up.

In a study released in the *Journal of Personality and Social Psychology* in October 20014, undergraduate students from the University of Amsterdam were studied regarding the effect of happiness and anger in negotiations.

The experiment was designed to test which emotion led to certain results. They were testing anger compared to happiness, compared to no emotion.

The participants were also tested for their need for cognitive closure. They were split between high need and low need.

The participants were then blindly assigned to different sections testing different variables. They were asked to make demands to their counterpart and a computer would mediate their negotiation.

The study results show that negotiators tend to make lower level demands to angry opponents compared to a happy counterpart. This research indicates that when you display worry or disappointment, the other side will make larger concessions. This also triggers the other party to compensate.

But please understand that there are limits to this. While this research does indicate the strong mood, it has to be rooted in something defensible.

Because the other party can easily say, "Why are looking disappointed and worried when you are actually getting a good deal?" They will then make their case. You have to be able to make your case.

So just simply mimicking disappointment and worry in the hopes that it would trigger compensatory behavior from the other side is not always guaranteed.

Another approach you can take involves reasonable anger. This is taking things to the next level, obviously.

Generally speaking, if you are dealing with a counterpart who has solid BATNA, emotional tricks are a little bit more dicey. However, if they are kind of unsure about their BATNA or their initial bargaining positions, you can push the envelope with strong emotions within reason.

This is where anger comes in. But it has to be reasonable.

In a 2006 study in the *Journal of Experimental Social Psychology*, researchers at Leiden University in the Netherlands, were testing whether angry messages or happy messages have an impact on computer-mediated negotiations.

During the negotiations, participants got happy or angry messages from computer-generated opponents. The researchers found that angry messages got more concessions than happy messages.

However, there are limits to this. Because when the message involved anger at an action taken, the other party is more likely to concede. However, when the anger is directed at the person, they gave less concessions compared to when the computer released messages that conveyed happiness towards the person.

When you take all these studies together, the key is to draw a distinction between being emotional about the person you're dealing with and their behavior.

It's okay. Most people are able to understand that you are upset about their behavior, but you're not upset at them.

So, if you're able to delineate the two, then this will give you a negotiation advantage.

Step by Step Guide to Using Proper Moods During Negotiations

Step #1: Display a positive mood in the beginning

Be friendly, smile, shake hands, offer a seat, and provide small gestures indicating goodwill.

Step #2: Show a positive mood throughout the negotiation process

Be hopeful. Look hopeful. Project hope and positive anticipation.

Step #3: When necessary, exhibit signs of disappointment

If the negotiation is not headed your way, express your disappointment.

Now, please understand that if you are dealing with somebody that you're in a long term business relationship with or a long time personal relationship with, this is usually not a good approach because this can easily come off as personal.

So please understand the difference. Use this tool only when warranted.

Step #4: Use appropriate anger based on evidence

If something comes up during the negotiation that would warrant justifiable anger on your part, then that's fine. This is the key.

Focus on what the other party is doing or what they are producing. Do not focus your anger on them as people and individuals.

For example, if you don't like a specific stipulation in a contract, express your anger that you don't like the condition. You don't think it applies. You think that it's too heavy. You think that it has too many negative effects. That's fine because you're just focusing on the terms and conditions.

On the other hand, if you say, "You guys are being unfair. You're trying to squeeze me. You guys are evil," then you're going to be stepping on toes. You're being overly emotional and you have personalized it and, chances are, you're making enemies.

I hope you can spot the difference. When you're expressing anger just like with disappointment, focus on behavior.

Also, it makes sense to use this technique only if you just met the other party or it's a relatively new relationship. But if you've done business with the other party for a very long time, this is not a productive approach.

Step #5: Despite showing negative emotions during negotiation, be respectful throughout

This is how people would know you are a professional. It's okay to have strong emotions, especially if it's just focused on certain terms or behavior of the other party, but not the actual person of the other party.

As long as you remain respectful and you don't attack people personally, they may come back to the table again in the future for another deal. You also increase the chances that this current negotiation will not fall apart.

Chapter 8: Create an Anchor and Make that First Impression

It's always a good idea to make the first offer. You end up "anchoring" the other party. They have a frame of reference as to the value or the context of your negotiation.

In the course of negotiation, you might stray very far from the initial offer, but it still has an effect. It creates context for the whole negotiation.

In fact, it would be fair to say that the negotiation really is a conversation about the first offer you made. Why? This is called the "first mover advantage."

Generally speaking, the negotiator who takes the initiative to make the first offer tends to get the better deal.

While this is most common in Western countries, it is effective in other cultures of the world. It's all about establishing context, but this takes initiative.

In an August 2013 article published in the journal *Personality and Social Psychology Bulletin*, researchers were studying whether the first mover advantage is a strictly Western phenomenon.

The study focused on 62 senior government officials recruited from Thailand's Ministry of Finance. These individuals were enrolled in an executive class negotiation course. They were split up between buyer and seller roles.

The whole premise of the negotiation is the sale of a pharmaceutical plant. Buyers were told their BATNA. They can build a brand-new plant for $25 million.

Sellers were given their BATNA as well. They could strip the plant and parcel out the equipment and sell it for a neat profit of $17 million.

Accordingly, there is a bargaining zone of $8 million created. Anything past this, then it wouldn't make sense for the other party to negotiate. Anything within this zone would be profitable for both parties.

Interestingly enough, when both parties were sent out to negotiations, the Western style phenomenon of making the first offer proved relevant. According to the study results, sale prices were higher when the sellers took the initiative to make the first offer compared to buyers.

This shows that even though Thailand has a strictly Eastern culture and business orientation, it is not immune to the Western phenomenon of first mover advantage.

One key element of first mover advantage involves the offer price. When making your first offer, start high. This gives you a lot of room to move.

For example, if you know that the value of whatever it is you're selling is $25, start out with $30. When the other person tries to negotiate you down, you end up where you wanted to be anyway.

Don't start out at the value you know. Start high. When you're aggressive, you are able to still give concessions and make the other party feel good while at the same time reaching your target price or something close.

You may also ask for a high range from the other side. This gives you a cushion as well.

Now, keep in mind, though, that when you give a range offer, this doesn't always work because you may be thinking that you're doing this out of goodwill and you're trying to make them comfortable so they can see the win-win situation.

But the problem is, you can bet that they will go with the lower end of that range so make sure that that range is still profitable to you.

Generally speaking, the more precise your anchor, the higher the chance your counterpart will settle somewhere close to that number.

Also, when you come up with a precise number for your anchor, it makes you look more decisive. It tends to push the other side to clearly look at their BATNA and see the best that they can come up with.

So, this is not clear cut. In certain situations, a range would make more sense. But you really have to play it by ear because, in most cases, the more precise your opening offer is, the better it would be for you.

Indeed, in a study published in the *Social Psychology and Personality Science Journal* in December 2013 showed that when sellers increased the precision of their offer, the anchoring effect of their first offers tended to be stronger.

The study involved 120 sellers in an online marketplace. The experiment actually had many different factors that it was measuring. First, it was focusing on how extreme the anchor is, whether it's high or low.

It is also paying attention to the precision of the anchor. Was it highly precise, somewhat precise, or open-ended?

The negotiators were then asked to give an offer and email it to the sellers. And as the email negotiations proceeded, it turned out that when the buyer made a low first offer, this led to lower final sales prices. But this depends on how precise and extreme their offer was.

When you increase the precision of your first offer and you follow it up with just as precise offers, the anchoring effect of your first offer is strengthened. Compare it to more open-ended offers, the sellers tended to assimilate more of the offers that are highly precise.

Another great way to negotiate using the anchoring effect is to tighten your ranges. While ranges can be effective, it has to be precise.

For example, if you really want to get paid $60,000 for your product, don't say, "I'll take anywhere from $55,000 to $60,000." It also doesn't make sense for you to say "$58,000 to $63,000."

The better approach would be to zero in on $60,000 and then go up, let's say, $60,000 to $65,000.

When you do that, you're basically just asking for $60,000 in a roundabout way. You're more likely to get that instead of something lower if you provided the range that starts off with a figure that's lower than $60,000.

Step by Step Procedures for Anchoring Effectiveness

Step #1: When making an initial offer, start high

Put your fears aside. Stop worrying that if you start out with a strong price that the other side will get scared off. Just start with a high price. This will enable you to give concessions by going down in price and still end up where you want to be.

Compare this with starting low and then having to push and convince the other party to give you more. Negotiating up is much harder than negotiating down.

Step #2: If you want to quote a price range, be precise and start at your target price

The key is to root your anchor in your target price. So, when you're giving a range and your target price is $50,000, start with $50,000 and give a range to

$55,000. Your counterpart is more likely to stick to that range and give you something more, especially if your real price is $50,000.

Step #3: If your counterpart takes the initiative and makes the first offer, focus on their anchor by getting rid of your own anchor

Instead of just trying to replace what they said with your anchor, just say, "What they want is just too much. You have to move. You have to give some concession. You're asking for too much or you're paying too little."

Step #4: Replace their anchor with your own if they're not conceding enough

If the other party made the first offer and they're not moving, throw out your own anchor. Just say, "Hey, let's look at my offer and see where it goes."

This changes the dynamic and flow of the negotiations and can lead to a better outcome, provided you can back up those numbers and you are behaving reasonably.

Chapter 9: How to Frame Your Offer the Right Way

If you're an effective negotiator, the deals that you negotiate will always be win-win solutions. This is the hallmark of a really great negotiator. There's something in it for you and there's something in it for the other side.

In fact, the best deals are win-win solutions, not just because everybody walks away with optimal results, but they're more likely to do business with each other in the future. That is the ultimate victory, because when you create a win-win situation, you build trust. Of all the other people, your counterpart can cut a deal with, you deliver.

You are able to give them what they're looking for while getting what you came for. They're more likely to want to seek you out than take a chance with somebody else who might not deliver the same results. While there's a possibility that they may get a better deal elsewhere, there's also a lot of risk.

When it comes down to it, most people are risk averse. We'd rather go with something that we already know. Keep this in mind when trying framing your offer. It has to be a win-win situation.

Please understand that the way you position your offer will greatly impact whether the other party will think they stand to gain or lose. That's how important it is. This is why you can't just do this on autopilot.

You can't assume that since you have the best price, that you just lay out the price, and everything will fall into place. That's assuming too much. That's assuming that the other party will clearly see the value you bring to the table.

Please understand that people fall for bad deals all the time. You may have the best deal in town, there's no doubt about that. But you have to put in the effort to position it as such. Otherwise, you shouldn't be surprised if the other party somehow, some way is convinced that somebody else has a better deal.

Successful framing is crucial. It's all about laying out options to your counterpart. These have to be manageable options. These have to be clear. And at the end of the day, these options must demonstrate whether the other side stands to gain or lose.

They can lose if they don't take your deal. They stand to gain tremendously if they take your deal. Seems pretty basic, right? But it all depends on the specifics of the agreement you're negotiating over. It's also a good idea to present several options at once.

The Power Of The Contrast Effect

When you present several offers at the same time, you're essentially lining up different options you're offering to the other party. This appeals to their psychological need to look at the best deal. Which of the options make them feel that they are getting away with the best possible outcome?

All of us have this built-in psychological need to come away with the best option. Knowing that this is the case, you have to arrange your options in such a way that the other party is more likely to pick the option that you want them to pick.

In a November 2011 study, published in the journal Psychological Science, researchers found that when a single word in a message is changed, it drastically impacted the behavior of people reading that message. The study involved healthcare professionals who were asked to wash their hands.

The researchers put up 66 dispensers which were made available to nurses and doctors in a hospital. They would then measure the amount of gel and soap used during the 2-week observational period.

They tested 2 signs: The first sign focused on personal consequences to the person being reminded. It read, "Hand hygiene prevents you from catching diseases." The contrasting sign focused on the effect on patients. It read, "Hand hygiene prevents patients from catching diseases." Finally, they also put a third sign which is the control message, and it read, "Gel in, wash out."

Each of the signs were randomly assigned to each of the 66 dispensers. Please note that there was only one-word difference between the personal consequences and the patient consequences sign. After the two-week observation period, the team weighed the amount of gel and other items left in the dispensers.

When comparing the amount of product use before and after the signs went up, the researchers concluded that when the sign focused on the consequences to the patient, hand hygiene product usage went up. On the other hand, dispensers that had the sign warning about personal consequences as well as the control sign, didn't show any change in usage.

This experiment shows that just changing one word can alter the convincing power of a message. This is all about framing. When you frame your offer, be careful with each and every word. They have a strong impact. They can make your offer look more attractive or easier to resist.

Use clear and manageable choices

One of the worst ways to come to an agreement is to bombard the other party with all sorts of options. If they have a long laundry list of choices to make, don't be surprised if they take a long time, or they don't make any decision at all.

Obviously, people don't want to make a mistake. We are, after all, dealing with their hard-earned money. Make the process easier for them by offering manageable choices. While people talk a good game about being presented with a lot of options, when it comes down to it, people actually would rather have fewer choices rather than more.

In a study that came out in January 2000 published in the journal Personality And Social Psychology, researchers wanted to test the longstanding assumption that when people have a lot more choices to choose from, they're more motivated to make a decision.

They set up a series of experiments. In one experiment, they put up a jam-tasting booth in a gourmet food store. In one weekend, shoppers were invited to taste six different jam options. The next weekend, shoppers were offered 24 different jams to taste test.

All the jams on offer were available for purchase. While the larger number of jams got a lot more people interested to try them out at the tasting table, these individuals tasted the same amount of jams as the previous weekend where they only had six options to choose from.

Interestingly enough, 30% of the people who were given only six jam options to buy ended up buying a jar. However, of those who were exposed to 24 types of jams, only 3% bought. This research concludes that when given an offer, it has to be manageable to the other side. You can't overwhelm them with so many options and so much complexity. They tend to freeze.

So while they do enjoy what you have to offer, they're less likely to make a decision. When framing your offer during negotiations, make the choice as manageable to the other side as possible. You have to do this despite the fact that people normally say, "Give me as many choices as possible. Give me your whole list." or "I want to see all that you have to offer."

They can do that, and they do, but if you follow through with that, you're not doing yourself any favor because they end up being overwhelmed. So keep it simple. Try to boil down your best deals or offers into a small manageable number.

These have to have enough contrast with each other so as to make it easy so people will have an easier time choosing among them.

Use multiple equivalent simultaneous offers or MESOs

This technique involves putting together several proposals that you think are equal and valid. They are all equally important to you. You then present it to the other side. When you do this, you show your hand to the other party.

You tell them in so many ways that by offering them these options, what issues are most important to you? The way they react, on the other hand, reveals what their priorities are. This is basically a way of reading each other in terms of priorities, and an agreement can be crafted based on which options matches which priority.

Of course, you have to do this within the framework of manageability. You can't just come up with so many different proposals that you think are equally valuable to you, but it ends up confusing the other side. You have to boil them down into a manageable number.

By offering multiple options, you're likely to increase the counterpart's satisfaction with one of the offers, and this leads to a higher chance that both of you will come to an agreement.

Step-by-step procedures for effective offer framing

Step #1 : Frame your offer based on your goals

The first thing that you need to do is to pay attention to the outcome that you desire. This is fundamental; you have to start here. You can't just create an offer because you want to please the other side. That's not going to work.

You have to focus on what you're getting out of it. What is the outcome that you are shooting for? And then from there, frame your offer. It's important to step through the issues that are involved with your goals.

For example, you're obviously looking to maximize profit, while at the same time, you're trying to increase the likelihood that this person or this company will do business with you again in the future. There's also the possibility that they would spread the word about your business.

So you have to balance these competing issues so you can come up with an offer that meets many different outcomes.

Step #2 : Provide the best possible options

The key here is to look at your offer and see the likelihood that your counterpart will find value in the option. In other words, is there a common ground for both of you to concede and walk away happy? This takes a little bit of research and initiative.

You can't just say, "Well, this is the price, I'm just going to lay it out." There has to be an opportunity for a common ground there.

Step #3 : Present the offer in manageable terms

When you're making an offer, present it in a way that's easy to understand and doesn't have too many moving parts. The more options you bombard the other party with, the less likely you will get to yes. Why? They might see the value in what you have to offer, but you have so many things to offer that you end up confusing them.

When people are faced with a lot of options, and are confused, they are more likely to just hesitate. As the old saying goes: When in doubt, stay out. Make it simpler for the other side. Make it easier for them to come to an agreement by easily seeing the value of the different offers you bring to the table, and by reducing the amount of options.

Step #4 : When your counterpart puts up resistance, refrain the issue quickly

If the other side puts up an objection, pivot and ask them, "How can we improve the situation? How can I improve this offer?" The key is to get to the root of their objection. Are they saying that it costs too much money? Are they saying that it's going to take too long, or it's too soon? What is the issue?

And see if you can concede on that while compensating on another level. For example, they say it's too expensive. You can re-frame by saying, "Okay, I can lower the per unit price, but can you agree to a larger volume? Or can you agree to a subscription or recurring purchase?"

There are many ways to play this. The key is not to stop at No, or to get distracted and sidetracked by objections. Objections can and do come, expect them. What's important is that you are able to pivot and adjust. You cannot just get blindsided and end up putting up a fight or otherwise giving off signals that derail negotiations.

Chapter 10: The Best Time To Give A Counter-Offer

Let's get one thing clear; counter-offers are absolutely necessary to any kind of negotiation. In fact, most negotiations usually don't end with the ideal deal either side desired. The deal that they walk away with isn't usually the deal that they had in mind when they came to the negotiation table.

Countering your counterpart's offer is crucial to any kind of effective negotiation preparation. Believe it or not, learning how to counter can and often leads to a better deal. You just have to be prepared. You just have to know how to play the game.

The key to effective counter-offers involves reading the other party correctly. Did you know that when the other party makes the offer, and you become silent for a short period of time, the silence becomes overbearing for them? It's not unusual for counterparts to respond to pauses in the negotiations, to increase their offer.

They may think that you have rejected their offer, so they're under a lot of pressure to increase their offer, because they don't want you to leave the negotiation table. On the other hand, if your counterpart gives you a flat 'No' on your offer, you might want to pause before giving your counter-offer.

You might want to give it a few minutes. This is crucial, because if you immediately concede and reduce your offer, it can motivate the other side to push you even harder. Make full use of the silence. Make silence your friend.

When you pause, tremendous pressure is put on the other side. Remember, they want something that you have. They wouldn't be at the negotiation table if they couldn't care less about what you bring to the table. They want what you have.

So when you turn down their offer, tremendous pressure is put on them, so don't be surprised if they quickly come back with a counter. But if they don't, let a few minutes pass, and then tell them about your counter.

How to handle resistance

When you make an offer and the other party resists, be ready to adjust your offer. This is only possible if you already have a clear idea of your offer and the range in which you can move. If you are unclear on these, then you may get thrown off-track and you might not get the best deal.

You might end up with a less optimal deal, or you might end up paying more. So it's very important to adjust your offer properly. This is not just a simple matter of just taking some dollars off, or raising the offer a few percentages. This is not mechanical in nature.

Instead, you have to diagnose why they resisted. Ask the six journalistic questions of who, what, where, when, why, how. Try to deconstruct in your head what could possibly be the reason why they resisted your offer.

Once you have this, you can then ask them a series of questions. You can probe their motivations. For example, you can say, "I understand that you think that this price is too high, or that this may not be the option for you right now, but please tell me, what is the most important thing for your company right now? What are your top priorities currently?"

When they give you the answer to these types of questions, you can make an educated guess as to what their mindset is. This allows you to figure out what their priorities are and craft together a solution that meets or fits those priorities.

Interestingly enough, negotiators with less bargaining power are able to use such diagnostic questions to create a positive impression in their counterpart. First of all, you establish that you're willing to deal. It also shows that you are willing to look at their priorities and what's important to them, and craft your offer accordingly.

This makes you look more trustworthy and easier to work with. You're not just there to sell or to buy.

Step-by-step procedures for making counter-offers

Step #1: Be Clear On Your Bottomline

This is crucial; while most deals have a lot of room to move, pay close attention to what your absolute limit is. This is the absolute base price. If you're selling, you can't accept anything lower than this. When you're buying, you cannot accept anything higher than this.

This has to be crystal-clear in your mind. Otherwise, you can lose quite a bit of money on this deal.

Step #2: Ask open-ended questions that shed light on your counterpart's offer or counter-offer

Ask diagnostic questions why they are making such an offer, or why they countered that way. This shows you their priorities. This also shows you what factors they're weighing, and this would inform you as to where you can reposition your offer in the form of counter-offer.

Step #3: Pause before you accept an offer

It's very easy to get excited when the other side gives you an offer that is above, or even way above your ultimate baseline. You might think that you already won. Wait, you can actually walk away with an even better deal just by shutting up right after they make the offer.

Don't be too eager to accept. Please understand that they are under a tremendous amount of pressure to close the deal. And if they made an offer already, this means that they are really interested and they would like to get this over with.

With you silent, they are under the impression that you may walk away, and this puts a tremendous amount of pressure on them, so they might even double-down or enhance their initial offer. As handsome as their offer is currently, but you shutting up, you might get away with an even more impressive deal.

Step #4: If the counter-offer matches your intended deal, take it

You can't play the game so long, and extend it so far that you end up losing out at the end. Lock in once the other side presents the deal you came for. This means that you shouldn't just counter just for the sake of countering. This means that you shouldn't let your ego get in the way, and push you to make a pointless counter to try to get a better deal.

You already won. Maybe you'll get a better deal if you just remain silent, and then they would be under a lot of pressure to sweeten the deal, but that's the best you can hope for. Other than that, if you counter, you might talk your way out of another wise, awesome deal.

Conclusion

Negotiation is a very important life skill. It applies to all areas of your life. Read the tips and strategies outlined in this book so you can become a better negotiator. While you may not necessarily be wheeling and dealing to cut billion-dollar real estate deals. These skills enable you to become a better person.

You become a better person by gaining people's respect and by being a more effective communicator. At the very least, people aren't walking all over you and taking advantage of you. You are able to communicate clearly and get concessions from others.

Please understand that in many areas of our lives, we are working towards certain common goals. Unfortunately, there will be clashes of egos. There will be people with ruffled feathers, and you may end up stepping on toes. This requires expert negotiation.

But with the right negotiation skills, and a very strategic mindset, you set yourself up for becoming a more successful person across the board.

Copyright © 2019 by Nick Anderson

All rights reserved. No part of this book may be reproduced in any form without permission in writing from the author.

No part of this publication may be reproduced or transmitted in any form or by any means, mechanical or electronic, including photocopying or recording, or by any information storage and retrieval system, or transmitted by email or by any other means whatsoever without permission in writing from the author.

DISCLAIMER

While all attempts have been made to verify the information provided in this publication, the author does not assume any responsibility for errors, omissions, or contrary interpretations of the subject matter herein.

The views expressed are those of the author alone and should not be taken as expert instruction or commands. The reader is responsible for his or her own actions.

The author makes no representations or warranties with respect to the accuracy or completeness of the contents of this work and specifically disclaims all warranties, including without limitation warranties of fitness for a particular purpose. No warranty may be created or extended by sales or promotional materials. The advice and recipes contained herein may not be suitable for everyone. This work is sold with the understanding that the author is not engaged in rendering medical, legal or other professional advice or services. If professional assistance is required, the services of a competent professional person should be sought. The author shall not be liable for damages arising here from. The fact that an individual, organization of website is referred to in this work as a citation and/or potential source of further information does not mean that the author endorses the information the individual, organization to website may provide or recommendations they/it may make. Further, readers should be aware that Internet websites listed in this work might have changed or disappeared between when this work was written and when it is read.

Adherence to all applicable laws and regulations, including international, federal, state, and local governing professional licensing, business practices, advertising, and all other aspects of doing business in any jurisdiction in the world is the sole responsibility of the purchaser or reader.

Printed in Poland
by Amazon Fulfillment
Poland Sp. z o.o., Wrocław